The Governor's Palace

The Governor's Palace

The Williamsburg Residence of Virginia's Royal Governor

By Barbara Carson

The Colonial Williamsburg Foundation
Williamsburg, Virginia

Library of Congress Cataloging-in-Publication Data

Carson, Barbara.
    The Governor's Palace.

    1. Governor's Palace (Williamsburg, Va.) 2. Interior
decoration—Virginia—Williamsburg. 3. Williamsburg
(Va.)—Buildings, structures, etc. 4. Governor's Palace (Williamsburg,
Va.)—Pictorial works. 5. Interior decoration—Virginia—Williamsburg
—Pictorial works. 6. Williamsburg (Va.)—Buildings, structures,
etc.—Pictorial works.
I. Title.
F734.W7C343   1987   975.5′4252   86-33413
ISBN 0-87935-120-9
ISBN 0-87935-121-7 (pbk.)

Book design: Vernon Wooten.

Photograph on pp. 64–65 reprinted by permission from *House Beautiful,*
© March 1986. The Hearst Corporation. All rights reserved.
William P. Steele, photographer.

Printed in the United States of America

Photographic credits: Kevin Burke, Frank Davis, Charles Lauson, Taylor Biggs
Lewis, Jr., Hans Lorenz, Gerry Rossner, Dan Spangler, Delmore Wenzel,
and Warren Winchester. Louis Luedtke did the architectural rendering of the
Governor's Palace.

Acknowledgments

Thanking the seven people who directly helped me with this project is both a professional obligation and a personal pleasure. However, to stop with that small number would overlook the indirect debt I owe many others. I hope this book clearly communicates a sense of the scale and the complexity of the scholarship that stands behind these pages. A team of dedicated and knowledgeable specialists, some with small armies of assistants, labored to refurnish the Palace building, to study the role of the royal governor in Virginia, and to prepare an interpretive story to present to visitors touring the building. Most of this happened before the spring of 1981 when the Governor's Palace reopened. Some of it is an ongoing effort. Eventually most of the principal scholars will write in detail about their areas of expertise. In all this I have been a reader and listener, lately arrived and absorbing the perspective and information of others before writing about their work in my own way.

Shortly before the Governor's Palace was to reopen, the staff realized that the general public might like to know more about the project than could be presented in a guided tour. A publication for the general reader would also be a permanent memento of what everyone was confident would be a highlight of a visit to Colonial Williamsburg. Few specialists take pleasure in writing about the work of other specialists, in balancing and synthesizing diverse studies. So the assignment was left to someone else, and I am grateful to Joseph N. Rountree, director of publications, for asking me. After I read hundreds of pages of typed reports and listened to hours of instruction taped for the interpretive staff, he helped me define the scope of the effort, and he has been warmly supportive as the manuscript was revised and edited. When words failed me, I turned to Cary Carson and Alvin Handleman to help clarify my thoughts and express them succinctly. In conversations that were fun and all too brief, Patricia Gibbs taught me much about the household staff and working relationships at the Palace. Many Colonial Williamsburg staff members read and commented on all or part of the manuscript at various stages; two were particularly conscientious. For several years John Hemphill has studied the political aspects of colonial governance. He worked hard to have this brief account accurately reflect his learned perspective. Graham Hood, vice president and chief curator, was the intellectual and inspirational leader for the Foundation-wide effort. In thoughtful comments, particularly on matters of taste and design, he tried to adjust my emphasis so the text better reflects the knowledge he and his staff have accumulated about the Palace, its furnishings, and the lives of the various governors. Patricia G. Maccubbin, audiovisual librarian, helped assemble the photographs. Finally, Donna Sheppard, editor/writer in Colonial Williamsburg's Department of Publications, supervised the transformation of a typed manuscript into an illustrated book, a truly complicated task, while Vernon Wooten was responsible for the design and production.

Those talented and dedicated individuals who contributed to the Palace refurnishing include: Desiree Caldwell Armitage; John C. Austin; Linda Baumgarten; John Bertalan; John D. Davis; Joan Dolmetsch; Hunter Earhart; Christopher Gilbert; Margaret Gill; Liza Pitzer Gusler; Wallace B. Gusler; Leroy Graves; Mack Headley; Roger Hedstrom; Tom Helme; Mary Hoffschwelle; Graham Hood; Brock Jobe; Mildred B. Lanier; Hans Lorenz; Jonathan Poston; Sumpter T. Priddy III; Margaret Beck Pritchard; Simon Redburn; Sue Bratt St. Amant; and Albert Skutans.

The Governor's Palace at Williamsburg

 ou are about to tour the reconstructed Governor's Palace at Colonial Williamsburg. By comparing it with today's White House, you may more easily understand the appearance of the building and its furnishings and the activities of its former occupants and visitors. In the eighteenth century the Palace, both home and office building, impressed people as the symbol of the authority of executive government. Today it is a shrine honoring the past, a storehouse of treasures, and a museum of living history. Welcome to the Governor's Palace.

Stepping through the front door, you step back in time two hundred years; you step into a "total picture" of the past as it existed on the eve of the American Revolution. "Total picture" means not only the appearance of the building and its furnishings but also the living standards, working conditions, and social hierarchy of the household, from the scullery maid to the butler to the royal governor, who officially represented the British government in the colony. The richness of the documentary evidence concerning the Palace's household organization and furnishings comes from sources as disparate as an inventory compiled by a faithful butler and a floor plan drawn by Thomas Jefferson.

This book discusses recent intensive scholarship undertaken by the Colonial Williamsburg Foundation. It explores the history of the Palace, which began in 1699 when the Virginia government, after the fiery destruction of the capitol building at Jamestown, decided to move to a new site named in honor of King William III.

Norborne Berkeley, Baron de Botetourt, served as governor of Virginia from 1768 to 1770. After his death, the House of Burgesses voted funds for a memorial statue of the popular executive, which the London sculptor Richard Hayward executed in 1772–1773. Erected in the piazza at the Capitol, it is one of only four such public statues known to have been in the colonies before the Revolution. Courtesy, College Archives, Swem Library, College of William and Mary.

The Royal Governor and Colonial Government

urprising as it may seem, between 1705 and 1768 the royal governor—the man who linked two governmental organizations, one in Virginia, the other in England, the man who headed the civil, military, judicial, fiscal, and religious branches of colonial government—neither lived in nor governed Virginia. The royal governors were busy English noblemen with responsibilities and interests elsewhere. They collected their salaries and met their official obligations as governor by appointing paid lieutenants; however, local usage in Virginia, which will be followed in these pages, identified the responsible official as the "governor."

As the representative of the royal prerogative, the governor had broad powers. He presided over the Council, an appointed advisory body of twelve or thirteen colonial citizens, and he called into session the elective body, the House of Burgesses, whose deliberations he had the right to terminate. In theory, the governor's position implied influence and authority. He was the most important person in the colony, and his position was acknowledged in many ways: he lived in a palace, he traveled in a carriage emblazoned with the arms of Virginia, he was referred to as "His Excellency" or "His Honour," and he was the object of much bowing and curtsying, respectful salutations, and obsequious requests.

King William III (1650–1702) by Peter Lely. Stadtholder of Holland, William married his cousin Mary, the elder daughter of James II, and was crowned joint sovereign of Great Britain in 1689. Courtesy, Joseph and Margaret Muscarelle Museum of Art, College of William and Mary.

In practice, however, the position did not automatically convey effective power. In the colony, native-born Virginians devised stratagems at home and exercised influence abroad that gave them the unofficial means to pursue their own objectives, regardless of the governor's wishes. In England, of course, the monarch wielded ultimate authority, disallowing any colonial law that conflicted with English law. William III established a chain of command that functioned with but few changes from 1696 to the Revolution. Behind the king stood the Privy Council, which provided advice, and the Secretary of State for the Southern Department, who took executive responsibility. Routine matters between England and Virginia were handled by another advisory body, usually referred to as the Board of Trade. Thus the governor was responsible to his patron (the full governor), to the various advisors and executives, and to the monarch.

The governor's job was made more difficult by forces outside his control. Between 1716 when Alexander Spotswood first occupied the Palace and 1775 when John Murray, Earl of Dunmore, fled to the safety of a British warship, Virginia's population grew from over eighty thousand to half a million, and, as its numbers grew, Virginia became an ever more important unit in England's expanding political and commercial empire. This rapid growth in sixty years' time demanded more complex government. While the members of the House of Burgesses and the Council met these demands with increasing self-confidence, the monarchy met them by enacting stricter and more rigid controls.

Caught between the colony and the crown, the governor's personality contributed to his success or failure. Those governors who were inaccessi-

Queen Mary II (1662–1694) at-tributed to Godfrey Kneller. The eldest child of James II and his first wife, Mary ascended to the British throne with her husband, William, after the "Glorious Revolution" of 1688. Mary had died by the time Williamsburg was founded. Courtesy, Joseph and Margaret Muscarelle Museum of Art, College of William and Mary.

ble to petitioners and overeager to profit from land speculation, who were arrogant and antagonistic, did not win the colonists' esteem. On the other hand, those governors who understood the subtle difference between theoretical and actual power, who grasped the diplomatic nature of their roles, who met with petitioners, who were gracious in entertaining and generous to servants, colonial institutions, and the needy, earned the people's goodwill and occasionally their genuine affection.

Alexander Spotswood (1676–1740). The first governor to live in the Palace, he was responsible for much of the design of the building and gardens.

John Murray, Earl of Dunmore (1732–1809), was the last royal governor of the Old Dominion. Several objects in the Palace today belonged to Dunmore and were sold at auction after he fled before dawn one morning in June 1775, thus ending for all time British rule in Virginia. Courtesy, National Galleries of Scotland, Edinburgh.

Palace History: 1698-1782

he present Palace, like its eighteenth-century predecessor, dominates one end of a long, narrow green. A person standing at the opposite end sees three long vistas, each terminating in a large brick public building. Down Duke of Gloucester Street to the east lies the Capitol, to the west is the Wren Building of the College of William and Mary, and down the green to the north is the Governor's Palace. Governor Francis Nicholson deliberately planned these open, commanding perspectives when he laid out the town in 1699. Perspectives were then popular in baroque Europe where monarchs and their designers cleared the twisted narrow streets and jumbled buildings of congested disorderly medieval towns and created visually comprehensible cities with wide, straight streets, open areas, and classical buildings. For colonial Virginians the up-to-date arrangement of the new capital town of Williamsburg confirmed their past achievements and symbolized their optimistic view of the future.

In 1724, approximately four years after the Governor's Palace was completed, Hugh Jones described it as "a magnificent structure built at the publick expense, finished with gates, fine gardens, offices, walks, a fine canal, orchards, etc." Such a splendid building was meant to confer prestige and honor on the colony. Yet in 1698, when the Board of Trade in London

Ediall Hall in Staffordshire is an example of the Anglo-Dutch style popular in England following the restoration of Charles II.

The Governor's Palace was depicted in a detail from the so-called "Bodleian Plate" of circa 1740. This source figured prominently in the reconstruction of the building as it appears today.

began to pressure the colony to provide a permanent residence for the royal governors, the colonial government responded with faint enthusiasm. The Council purchased a piece of property, but the House of Burgesses demurred. The expense of building the new capitol delayed their willingness to meet the additional cost of an official residence. For eight years the burgesses dragged their feet. Finally, in 1706, they authorized two new taxes to provide three thousand pounds "for building ye Gouvernour a House." The authorization specified materials and dimensions, but little else. Details of the design probably evolved from consultations between a committee of Virginia gentlemen and Henry Cary, who was appointed to oversee the construction.

While the colony and the Board of Trade dickered over an official residence, royal governors lived in rented houses, accommodations hardly appropriate to their position. The British government paid a rent allowance for ten years during the long construction period. About 1716 the first governor moved into the still unfinished structure. Another four or five years passed before the last nail was hammered in the entire complex. During the building years the House of Burgesses periodically appropriated additional sums for furnishings, outbuildings, and gardens. Between 1705 and 1776 more than seven thousand pounds were spent on construction and a similar amount on repairs. These were large expenditures for that time.

The original building had rooms separated by a central corridor, a symmetrical facade, a pair of identical outbuildings flanking a forecourt, and formal gardens in the front and rear. The building's design was a combination of sixteenth-century Italian classicism and an older Netherlandish tradition characterized by steep-pitched roofs and red brick walls. The Italianate tradition was established throughout Europe by the writings and drawings of Andrea Palladio. The Dutch ideas came to England through commercial connections strengthened by the marriage of William, Stadtholder of Holland, to Mary, an English princess, and their joint succession to the

English throne in 1689. The amalgam of styles, now called Anglo-Dutch Palladianism, dominated English architecture in the late seventeenth and early eighteenth centuries. Although in England there are no buildings identical to the Palace, its general plan and appearance have many parallels in the modest but comfortable residences of prosperous merchants, country gentlemen, and clergymen. In the colonies, the Palace had no immediate prototypes and no immediate successors—no rival dimmed its splendor.

By the mid-1750s, however, its design was passé. New styles gave a new look to room decoration, furniture, fabrics, and accessories. Life styles had changed too. Well-bred people even in provincial communities were learning to enjoy large "assemblies" or "routs," as they called evening parties. In his popular English architectural book, *A Complete Body of Architecture* (1756), Isaac Ware explained that the new fondness for parties "brings in the necessity of a great room, which is opened only on such occasions. In houses which have been sometime built, and which have not an out of proportion room, the common practice is to build one to them."

Striving to keep up with current fashion, the colony significantly altered the Palace: several fireplace surrounds were replaced, the forecourt on Palace Green probably was reorganized, and a ballroom and supper room were added to the north elevation. An unusually large sum of money allocated for repairs in 1753 and 1754 establishes the date for these renovations, although no itemized

"The Cotillion Dance," engraved in England in 1771 by James Caldwell after a painting by John Collet, satirizes the dancing customs of the day.

accounts or specifications have been found. By paying for these costly additions, the colony signaled its readiness to provide the governor with a setting suitable for entertainments in the latest fashion.

For the next thirty years, the Palace received nominal improvements: royal portraits, wallpaper, chandeliers, coal grates, stoves. Then, with American independence, came neglect and destruction. Williamsburg briefly became the seat of the revolutionary government and the Palace became the official residence of the new commonwealth's governors. The first two, Patrick Henry and Thomas Jefferson, lived and worked there, apparently in much diminished splendor according to one observer who reported that "since the war [the rooms] are wholly defaced." In 1780 the Virginia legislature moved the capital to Richmond, and the Palace stood empty until 1781 when it was used as a hospital for the American army. On the night of December 22, 1781, the Palace caught fire and within a few hours "was absolutely consumed by . . . flames." Behind the flanking advance buildings only the ruined walls remained standing. In 1782 the state took action to clear the site, sold the bricks, and conveyed the property to the College of William and Mary, which sold off various parcels over the years. The pair of brick advance buildings became private residences. One had disappeared by the Civil War. Ruins of the other survived long enough to be recorded in early photographs.

A photograph taken shortly after the Civil War shows the ruins of one of the advance buildings, all that remained of the Palace complex.

Reconstructing the Palace

In 1926 when the Palace had been totally lost to view for over a century, Dr. W. A. R. Goodwin, a local Episcopal rector, persuaded John D. Rockefeller, Jr., that it was not unthinkable to turn back the hands of time. Goodwin believed that modern research techniques could be used to resurrect an entire eighteenth-century town. Their dream led to the creation of Colonial Williamsburg, where they set out "to restore the setting of great historical events, and recover the great object lesson in monumental town planning." The Capitol and the Governor's Palace were to be the principal gems of the restoration. Rockefeller was determined to reconstruct both completely, "preserving existing foundations wherever possible."

Five major sources of evidence helped the restoration architects bring back the Governor's Palace. A map of the town drawn by a French military cartographer shows Palace Green with its two bordering rows of trees and the main Palace block plus the ballroom wing, flanking advance buildings, and the principal dependencies. A measured floor plan drawn by Thomas Jefferson permits a closer look at dimensions and room arrangement and hints at structural changes made during the eighteenth century. An engraver's copperplate discovered in the Bodleian Library at Oxford University preserves the only known view of the front elevation as it appeared about 1740. The fourth important source is the inventory of personal possessions taken after the death of Governor Botetourt in 1770. Although other documents record some Palace furnishings—among them catalogs of the "standing furniture" owned by the colony, a partial inventory of Governor Francis Fauquier's possessions, and a list that accompanied Dunmore's petition for losses sustained when he fled the colony—the Botetourt inventory is far and away the most helpful because it gives the name of each room. These designations confirm the evidence of the Jefferson plan for the ground floor and provide additional clues about the disposition of rooms on the second and third floors. All these lists, especially Botetourt's inventory, were immensely valuable in furnishing the reconstructed Palace and in understanding how household life was organized. The last major source of information was the Palace itself. Although nothing survived above ground, underground the cellar walls, floors, foundations, and thousands of artifacts awaited discovery.

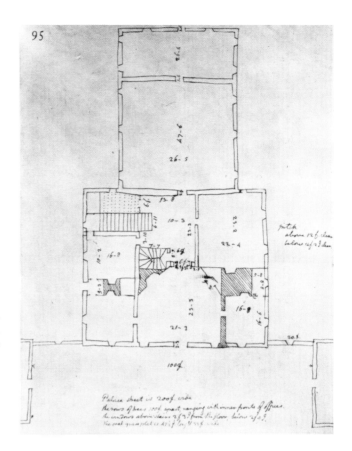

Thomas Jefferson's measured drawing of the Palace not only indicates the plan but also supplies dimensions of the rooms, ceiling heights, and wall thickness. Courtesy, Massachusetts Historical Society.

Archaeologists uncovered sections of the Palace's foundations during excavations in 1930. Note the similarity of the excavated foundations to Jefferson's plan of the Palace.

Excavation of the Palace site took place in the summer of 1930. Archaeologists found sections of the foundations and interior cellar walls standing several feet high, and these the architects carefully incorporated into the reconstructed building. Today they are clearly visible in the cellar storage area. When a building burns, much of the structure and its contents come crashing down into the cellar. The debris contains clues about building materials and artifacts, and sometimes the pattern of destruction allows careful investigators to identify where artifacts were located before the fire began. Archaeological detective work helped architects make decisions about the appearance of the reconstructed Palace. For instance, the discovery of many pieces of polished black and white marble in the rubble below the entrance hall left little doubt that stone pavers had floored

The excavated cellars appeared in a remarkable state of preservation with passageways, steps, doorways, and the lower portions of brick vaults intact.

that room. The excavation log for Friday, August 1, 1930, records the discovery of another feature: "Two pieces of carved marble were found . . . East side of building. Both pieces look like parts of mantel. One piece has a deer and other carving on it and the second piece branch of tree or shrub." These fragments and many other smaller pieces of pink, gray, and beige marble were used, jig-saw puzzle-like, to determine the appearance of a chimneypiece now installed in the parlor. The large carved fragments dug from the site were reset in the twentieth-century reproduction.

Just as the marble fragments assisted the architects, fragments of wine glasses, plates, and fancy tablewares were helpful to curators in furnishing the reconstructed Palace. Archaeological shards helped give specific form to generalized inventory references like "6 flowered wine glasses and 13 Hock glasses" or "35 plain wine Glasses."

The decision to reconstruct and eventually to furnish the Palace posed a difficult historical challenge. Although the evidence for its appearance was considerable, many questions remained unanswered and always would. Jefferson's sketch and the Bodleian engraving provided enough information for architectural historians to make valid generalizations, but modern-day

Fragments of carved marble (above) *found in the rubble below the east side of the building were used, jig-saw puzzle-like, to re-create the chimneypiece in the parlor.*

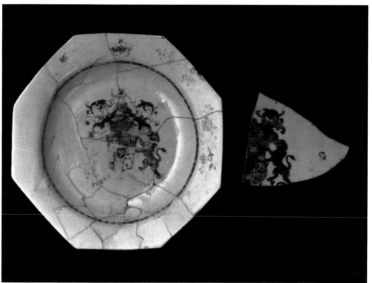

Fragments of many objects used in the Palace were found by archaeologists clearing its rubble filled cellars in 1930.

The stem of an English-made wine glass is from the period 1730–1745.

A creamware bottle cooler made in Staffordshire, England, about 1765–1770 is decorated with a transfer-printed design of birds and plants.

A creamware fruit basket has a decoration similar to that of the bottle cooler.

A porcelain plate made and decorated in China about the middle of the eighteenth century bears the arms of Lord Dunmore.

masons, carpenters, plasterers, and painters need specific instructions as to brick patterns, molded door surrounds, carved ornamentation, paint colors, and a thousand other details. Turning the limited historical evidence into working drawings and then into a physical reality required painstaking research and much educated guesswork. Restoration architects carefully studied existing eighteenth-century buildings. They took measurements. They noted the width of mortar joints and the style of scoring them. They counted windowpanes and measured their sizes. They took molding profiles, paint samples, and much much more. They then fitted all this information from comparable buildings into the framework of known facts about the Palace and thereby created a structure that for more than fifty years has impressed laymen and experts alike with the restoration architects' ability to recapture the ideas and practices of the original builders.

The reconstruction moved more swiftly than the original eighteenth-century building had. In 1934 the Governor's Palace was opened to the public. Initially it was unfurnished, and the bare rooms revealed little of the flavor of colonial life. Gradually, curators acquired representative antique furnishings, and hostesses organized an interpretive program for visitors. From the beginning, however, Colonial Williamsburg knew that both the furnishing scheme and the interpretive program would have to be open to new ideas. This was as it should be. Times change; visitors change; our knowledge and understanding of history change. The Palace Governor Spotswood built differed in the eighteenth century from the Palace of Gooch, of Fauquier, of Botetourt, and of Dunmore. The Palace today differs from the Palace of the 1930s. The trees have grown; more accurate furnishings have been found; the program for visitors takes new emphases and directions. Only by continuous research and evaluation can Colonial Williamsburg fulfill its educational objective to help people today better understand Virginia's colonial past.

The Palace was reconstructed at the head of Palace green behind the local school, which was torn down and rebuilt on another site.

Norborne Berkeley, Baron de Botetourt, as a young man. His death after only two years in office plunged Virginians into mourning.
Courtesy, His Grace the Duke of Beaufort.

Governor Botetourt and His Household at the Palace

n October 26, 1768, Norborne Berkeley, Baron de Botetourt, landed in Hampton, Virginia, and according to the Williamsburg newspaper "was saluted with a discharge of cannon . . . [He] set out about noon for this City, where he arrived about sunset. His Excellency stopped at the Capitol, . . . and having his Commissions read, was qualified to exercise his high office, by taking the usual oaths. His Excellency then . . . proceeded to the Raleigh Tavern, and supped there with his Majesty's Council. His Excellency retired about ten, and took up his lodgings at the palace."

By the late 1760s the increasing importance of Virginia's wealth to the Mother Country and the deteriorating relationship between them brought the governor's office into greater prominence. In the fall of 1768 the Stamp Act crisis was over but new taxes under the Townshend Acts aroused colonial protests. The British government anticipated trouble and knew the presence of a titled aristocrat as full resident governor of Virginia would flatter the colonists and increase the possibility of Britain's establishing effective control over the colonial government.

Lord Botetourt brought more than a fancy title and fine manners to this new post. He was superbly qualified to meet the challenge of governing Virginia. A bachelor in his middle fifties, Botetourt already had more than twenty years of experience in government and business. He was highly respected as a man of affairs despite financial difficulties that he hoped to reverse in Virginia. In the colony he quickly made a reputation for piety, fairness, generosity, and diligence in performing his sometimes difficult duties as governor. He stood firm in defense of the king's prerogative, as in 1769 when he dissolved the House of Burgesses following its denial of Parliament's right to levy taxes on the colonies. But he knew how to take away the sting of a rebuff. Privately he predicted that Parliament would repeal the taxes. He entertained his adversaries at the Palace. And he turned a blind eye to the ladies who came to a ball in his honor dressed in homespun gowns to dramatize their support for the nonimportation agreement. Treading a fine line between obeying English orders and showing sympathy for the colonists' position, Botetourt preserved his personal integrity at home and abroad. Horace Walpole thought all his "douceur to be enamelled on iron." Maybe it was, but it elicited genuine admiration from his servants who knew him best as well as from those Virginians who knew him only slightly. All mourned his sudden death in October 1770. He had governed less than two years; many believed he was the best governor Virginia had ever known.

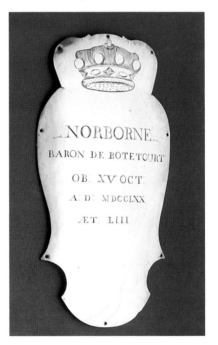

Invitations were issued for Lord Botetourt's elaborate state funeral on October 19, 1770. The ceremony and related expenses cost £700, a substantial amount for that day. Courtesy, Manuscripts and Rare Books Department, Swem Library, College of William and Mary.

Williamsburg silversmith William Waddill supplied this large silver nameplate and the silver handles for Lord Botetourt's coffin. At Botetourt's request, he was buried beneath the chapel at the college, where the governor had attended morning services daily. Courtesy, College Archives, Swem Library, College of William and Mary.

Lord Botetourt endowed the annual awarding of two gold medals as academic prizes at the College of William and Mary. Nathaniel Burwell of Carter's Grove received this medal in 1772 for excellence in moral philosophy.

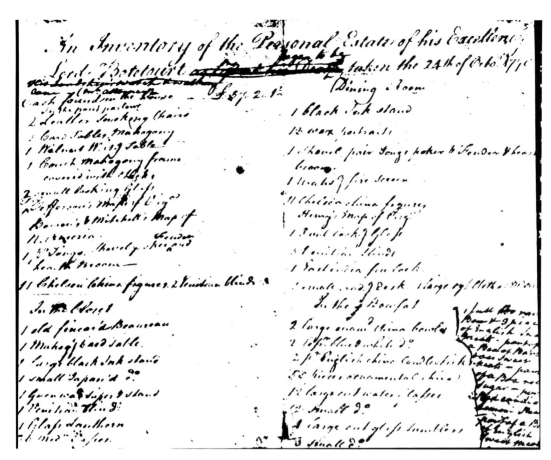

The inventory of Lord Botetourt's possessions with its room-by-room listing of over 16,500 items is the central document in the furnishing of the Palace. Courtesy, Archives Branch, Virginia State Library.

The colony's loss is our gain two hundred years later. Five days after Botetourt was buried with due pomp and ceremony, the administrators of his estate began to compile an inventory of his personal possessions. This document, begun on October 24, 1770, lists the contents of more than sixty rooms and storage areas in and around the Palace. Because the inventory takers itemized over 16,500 separate objects in the rooms where they found them, their lists provided Colonial Williamsburg's curators with excellent information for furnishing the Palace. This exhaustive compilation is supplemented by numerous letters, some written by Botetourt himself, others by various members of the household. There are also account books that tell about money collected and disbursed in the course of running the Palace. A "Dayly Account of Expenses" and "Ac-

The unicorn on this reproduction livery button was copied from Lord Botetourt's crest. Liveried servants wore the colors and often the heraldic devices of their masters.

1768
May 7.th

Will.m Fenlon

For Julere new Stuffing the
Seat of a Selle mending the } — 12 —
frame one new Caster

For a new hinge to a reeding desk — 4 6

For 3 Large print frames &
glasses & packing case } 1 10 —

For 6 Crimson Check Cases
to 6 stuffed back & Seat Cheax } 1 13 —

For 9 brass hooks & Several
jobs done — — — — } — 3 —

For new green Jammey to 2
Spring Curtons and mending } 1 5 —
them — — — — — }

20 For a bedside Carpet 2 yards
& ½ long } — 11 6

For 2 11/4 Linning quilts — 4 4 —

For 2 10/4 ditto — 3 16 —

Extensive accounts with London tradesmen illuminate details of Lord Botetourt's purchases for the Palace. Courtesy, His Grace the Duke of Beaufort.

count of Money received and disbursed . . . by William Marshman," Botetourt's butler, receipts for servants' wages, a tally of "Work Done with the Cart," and various kitchen accounts kept by the cooks are among the records that take historians behind the scenes to glimpse the workings of the governor's household. The initial survival of these records can be attributed to the deliberate thoroughness of William Marshman, who carefully bundled up Botetourt's possessions and sent them off to England. The ship carrying the personal property went down off Cape Henry; the safe landing of the other ship brought the documents to Botetourt's nephew and heir, the fifth duke of Beaufort. Continuous succession of that ducal family and the stability of their estate and manuscript collection have resulted in the preservation of the Williamsburg material.

Supplemental information regarding the furnishing of the Palace during Lord Dunmore's administration is provided by the schedule of losses he filed in 1784 for compensation, in part, for the possessions he left behind. PRO Audit Office 13, Loyalist Claims. Courtesy, Public Records Office, London.

Careful study of the documents shows that the Palace can only be understood as the nerve center of a conglomeration of other buildings, work areas, and estates. Quite properly, when Colonial Williamsburg rebuilt the Palace, it built not only the main house but two advance buildings, the kitchen, scullery, smokehouse, laundry, tool house, storehouses, privies, coach house, and stables. The Foundation also replanted approximately ten acres of pleasure gardens, which today contain the original icehouse. In the eighteenth century the Palace lands extended north to include about 150 acres of parkland with managed woods, grazing pasture, and cultivated farmland. Shortly before the Revolution, probably during Dunmore's governorship, the Palace lands were enlarged to about 364 acres. The colony also owned a 3,000-acre tract along the James River that the governor leased to tenants, the rents going toward his support.

In the eighteenth century, a footman stationed at the front door welcomed visitors to the Governor's Palace.

The cook and several helpers prepared tasty and attractive dishes in the kitchen, which is located in the service area to the west of the building.

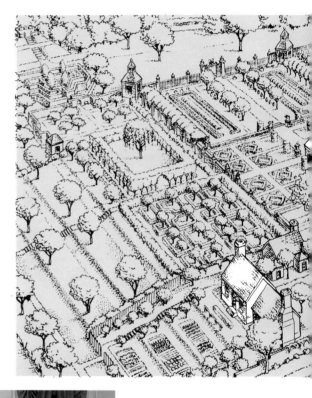

At the Governor's Palace, the dining room was a place to eat, to talk, and to conduct business. His lordship set a sumptuous table.

The butler supervised the governor's domestic staff and managed the entire household from his office in the pantry.

The stables and carriage house east of the Palace building served the transportation needs of the household.

The governor kept stocks of wine, beer, foodstuffs, and other supplies in the cellars.

To understand the household routines and business of government that took place in the Palace complex requires an awareness of more than the governor's official role as the king's representative and the appearance and function of the main Palace building. Lord Botetourt employed the services of what would seem to us to be a large household staff, some twenty to twenty-five people. Although its organization conformed to English practice, the number of servants was smaller than usual and included about twelve slaves. Botetourt initially brought most of his white servants with him from England. Six had been members of his staff in London or at Stoke Park in Gloucestershire. Most, including his faithful butler, William Marshman, remained in his lordship's service until his death. Their devotion to a single employer was uncommon. Domestic staffs usually turned over rapidly. Those servants hired specifically for the stint in Virginia were more typical. They remained on Botetourt's staff a short time only and were soon replaced by native Virginians.

Most people in the eighteenth century believed that God appointed each person to his own place in the stratified order of society. They believed, too, that everyone had an obligation to accept the position to which he was born and to fulfill its duties to the best of his ability. According to Robert Dodsley, servants were admonished to

> Repine not, O man, at the state of servitude; it is the appointment of God, and hath many advantages, it removeth thee from the cares and sollicitudes of life.
> The honour of a servant is his fidelity; his highest virtues are submission and obedience.
> Be patient therefore under the reproofs of thy master; and when he rebuketh thee, answer not again: the silence of thy resignation shall not be forgotten.

Today such precepts strike us as unimaginably demeaning and unacceptable. In the eighteenth century servants and masters alike regarded deference as basic to the social order and the conduct of daily life.

The servant-master relationship was unequal but reciprocal. Masters were reminded to "be just to thy servant, if thou expecteth from him fidelity; and reasonable in thy commands, if thou expecteth a ready obedience." For his English servants Botetourt was an exemplary master. "No Servant had ever heaped upon him such continual proofs of kindness from any Master," wrote Marshman after his death, "as I receiv'd from that Generous and Good Man." Botetourt seems not to have shown the same regard for all. Palace account books indicate that he followed local eighteenth-century disciplinary procedures when he occasionally hired Williamsburg's constable to flog black slaves.

Servants were distinguished by their relative positions within the serving hierarchy in large households like the Palace. A servant's status determined the type of work he did, where he slept, and where and what he ate. Botetourt's five upper servants—a butler, a land steward, a cook, a groom of the chambers, and a gardener—supervised the others—an undercook, two footmen, a coachman, a groom, several housemaids, gardener's assistants, stable hands, and farm hands. Running a large household in colonial times was a full-time operation. Botetourt's servants had many duties. Hours and hours of menial labor produced the scrubbed floors and polished fire grates, the starched and pressed linens for the liveried servants, the tasty and attractive dishes set on the dining table, the groomed horses and the oiled harnesses.

A servant's day began early and ended late. A footman, one of the lower servants, might, for example, rise about 5:30 A.M. He dressed first in work clothes, lighted the fires, and did messy work like polishing silver. These tasks completed, he washed and dressed in his livery before eating breakfast. Then there was the table to set and his master to rouse and wait upon. Apart from serving at table, his principal duties were to answer the door and to carry out the bidding of his master and the butler. His tasks were concluded only after they went to bed. Other servants' schedules were similar. The pace varied according to the time of day, the season of the year, or the master's special needs.

By working efficiently, Botetourt's comparatively small staff followed an established routine at the Palace. Special entertainments and seasonal activities required extra hands. Botetourt hired temporary help—both black and white—to prepare and serve at dinners and balls, to provide music for special events, and to work on the farm and in the gardens when the need was pressing. In addition, Botetourt brought three artisans with him from England. A blacksmith, carpenter, and upholsterer-gilder remained on his staff for about a year. After they left his personal service and opened their own businesses in Williamsburg, Botetourt's accounts show that he continued to hire these men for special work.

About three-quarters of the approximately sixty interior spaces specified in Botetourt's inventory were used as living quarters for servants, as work areas—the laundry, kitchen, pantry, and such—or as rooms for storage of all sorts of food and household paraphernalia. The cook and gardener were assigned their own rooms, perhaps in the west advance building. The head servant in Botetourt's household was William Marshman, butler and perhaps valet to his lordship. Curiously, no document indicates a separate room assigned to him. He may have slept in the pantry on the "Ticken couch" with "Mattrass boulster 3 blankets white quilt and red check

Seen from above, the Palace outbuildings form an enclosed service yard.

covering," although today this arrangement seems unsatisfactory for a man of his status.

Lower servants were accommodated according to their duties and wherever space could be found. The coachman and groom had rooms furnished with beds, but the chambers also doubled as tackrooms for the horse and carriage harness. Beds for others were to be found in several of the third floor rooms of the Palace. As a bachelor Botetourt had no family in Virginia. During his occupancy these attic rooms may well have been used by servants. At other times they may have been rooms for children and guests. Certainly some servants endured meager if not downright unpleasant accommodations. One wonders who used the "1 old mattress, 2 old blankets" that were the only contents of the "Small Room adjoining to

Items kept in the cellars included "6 Casks strong" and "6 ditto small Beers—unopened, 1 Barrel of Cranberries, 1 Hogshead Molasses Beer," and dozens of bottles of wine.

*Built-in shelves in the Palace
kitchen hold the "5 Tea Canisters[,] 2 round coffee canisters,"
and "Earthen sweet meat pots"
listed in the Botetourt inventory.*

[the] Poultry House." No accommodations specifically designated for slaves are mentioned in any of the Palace documents. Elsewhere in Williamsburg they slept above kitchens, stables, or other outbuildings. Probably the governor's slaves slept in similar locations at the Palace.

Status also determined what and where a servant ate. Lower servants waited on upper servants, who consumed leftovers from the governor's table. Historians think that the upper servants ate in the cook's bedchamber or in a servants' hall of uncertain whereabouts. Lower servants consumed older leftovers and simple fare in a second servants' hall. The slaves may have eaten there too, but because Virginia custom separated blacks from whites at mealtimes, the Palace may have had still another dining place, perhaps the scullery.

Storage areas took up a lot of room in the Palace complex. Furnishings used seasonally or only occasionally in reception rooms or semiprivate areas show up in the inventory in storerooms or closets. For instance, the chimney board and blue moreen window curtains belonging to the dining room were found in a storeroom and a nearby closet. Storage areas in the cellars held foodstuffs, drink, and supplies such as tallow and spermaceti candles, a box of bottle corks and stoppers, and empty containers. "English moist sweet Meats," cranberries, molasses, brown sugar, pickled mangoes, white wine, claret, Burgundy, port, Madeira, brandy, champagne, ale, beer, and both Virginia and English cider stayed cool in the cellars. Other storerooms held a wider assortment of items—yard goods, carpet brooms, soap, starch, and ceramic, glass, and pewter tablewares in addition to sugar, tea, coffee, raisins, spices, "3 Cannisters flour of mustard," "a large Paper of Sarsaparilla," and on and on.

Storage had a significance for eighteenth-century life that differs from usual twentieth-century practice. Although by the 1770s Williamsburg was no longer a frontier outpost, the supply lines for luxury items like wine, imported cheeses, oranges, and spices were not always reliable. A good reserve insured against the weeks when the right ship did not arrive in port. Storage also was security. Today we protect possessions by locking doors and windows around the perimeter of our houses. In a large eighteenth-century household, particularly one like the Palace, securing the outer walls was impractical. Tradesmen, guests, servants, and casual help needed freedom to come and go. Locked storage rooms, cellars, closets, and even pieces of storage furniture prevented serious theft and petty pilferage. "Always take care to keep your doors and your cuberts lockt where you have any charge" was one instruction a Scottish lady gave her butler.

The dining room was an elegant setting for political lobbying and discussions. The diplomatic Botetourt honored his guests by serving them from his extensive silver. The governor was the only person in Virginia who had enough sterling plates, flatware, and dishes to serve an entire meal. Dessert eaten with "gilt Silver handled" knives and forks crowned the repast. Guests sipped Lord Botetourt's fine wines from one of his six gold cups.

The Palace Furnishings

The Palace was a public building in ways that we today find almost unimaginable. Planters, burghers, tradesmen, foreign travelers, Indians, sea captains, soldiers, and officials frequented the governor's residence on business that brought them even into the inner sanctum of his lordship's bedchamber. Consequently, the Palace was furnished almost entirely for show. And what furnishings they were! Polished steel arms, richly figured pieces of walnut and mahogany furniture, chairs upholstered in scarlet and crimson, dazzling cut glass chandeliers, exquisite porcelain garnitures, gilt tablewares, portraits, prints, and paintings. In all, over 16,500 objects, decorative and useful, were assembled at the Palace in 1770 when Governor Botetourt's death occasioned the taking of an

The Botetourt inventory contains rare colonial American references to Chelsea porcelain. Mantels in both the parlor and dining room held "11 Chelsea China figures."

At the end of the list of Lord Botetourt's personal possessions the inventory takers entered the "standing furniture" belonging to the colony. A Williamsburg-made chair with "Virgᵃ" stamped into the seat rail served as the prototype for this chair, one of a set in the parlor and pantry. The original chair is in the Daughters of the American Revolution Museum in Washington, D. C.

Also listed among the standing furniture was "1 Side Board wᵗʰ Marble Slab" in the dining room. This walnut example was made in Virginia about 1735 and represents furniture acquired by the colony for the official residence during the tenure of previous governors.

inventory. Today that document has enabled Colonial Williamsburg to re-create, as carefully as curators and historians know how, a world much less familiar than at first it may appear.

Visitors to the refurbished Palace see a superb collection of rare American and English antiques. Luckily, many of the objects can be associated with the eighteenth-century building. The firescreen in the dining room was once owned by Lord Botetourt. A larger number of furnishings were once owned by Lord Dunmore. After he fled from the Palace at the outbreak of the Revolution, the state confiscated his goods and sold them at auction. Some of the original purchasers prized this history and documented it or insured that their heirs kept the story alive as a family tradition. These items are the clock in the library, the desk and bookcase in the bedchamber over the dining room, and six of the chairs and one of the chair-back settees in the ballroom. The silver candlesticks in the parlor are engraved with Dunmore's arms and earl's coronet. They survived in the Dunmore family and were given by descendants to the Colonial Williamsburg Foundation. A much larger group of antique objects is made up of items probably not in the eighteenth-century Palace but virtually identical to those the documents specify. The maps, for instance, are authentic examples from the hands of the same surveyors, engravers, and printers. The thirteen authentic side chairs and one arm chair in the dining room are very similar to a privately owned example with a Dunmore history. Allan Ramsay's large royal portraits in the ballroom, the thirteen wax portraits in the dining room, much of the silver, many of the books, and other items stand in for similar originals.

The antiques in today's Palace are augmented by modern reproductions, mostly made in recent years by Colonial Williamsburg craftsmen. Achieving an authentic eighteenth-century appearance for the Palace interiors required reproducing large sets of chairs, brass candelabra, globe lamps, and eighteenth-century firearms be-

In his Analysis of Beauty *(1753), English artist William Hogarth described and illustrated the essence of beauty as "the waving line of variety," which could be seen in both natural and man-made objects.*

cause large numbers of matching antiques were not available at any price. Scarceness and a concern for preservation led also to the extensive use of reproduction textiles. Many yards of fabric are required to drape a bed, hang a window, or cover a set of chairs in the eighteenth-century manner. Antique examples of certain kinds of floor coverings—the painted floor cloth in the dining room, for example, or the woven carpets in several other rooms—survive rarely, sometimes only in fragments, and are too fragile to withstand display in a building visited by so many people. In each of these cases reproductions enhance the authenticity of the scene, making it more like the Palace the eighteenth-century governors knew.

The waving line could be balanced and graceful as in the Worcester jar above or in the cabriole legs of the table opposite. Alternatively, it could be energetic and tightly twisted as in the asymmetrical gilt bracket that represents the height of English rococo taste.

Producing curvilinear forms was more costly than making rectilinear ones. They required more raw material and extra labor. This Pembroke table is in the taste termed "neat and plain," meaning well-proportioned design and high quality wood and workmanship without extravagance.

The fashion for curvilinear lines implied an interest in motion and in three-dimensional or sculptural form. The curves of the legs continue up and around the spiraling ribs of the pedestal. The top tilts, and the alternating pattern of straight and curved molding moves the viewer's eye around its rim.

Each piece, antique or reproduction, was selected by curators in accordance with the Botetourt inventory, and each could tell a story all its own. Here there is only room for a selection of the most interesting and informative. Before touring the Palace one room at a time, a few general comments are in order to explain how the furnishings and their arrangement figured in the daily lives of governors.

Botetourt's inventory confirms the impression from other sources that the Palace did not come entirely unfurnished each time a new governor took up residence. In 1710 the colony authorized the expenditure of £250 for "buying necessary standing and ornamentall furniture for the said house, which furniture shall be provided in this country or sent for from Great-Britain." Other pieces of this so-called "standing furniture" were acquired later, for example, from the estate of former Governor Drysdale. By 1770 the colony owned twelve looking glasses distributed through the principal Palace rooms. Other government-owned equipment included prints, paintings, maps, and lighting fixtures. After the muskets, pistols, bayonets, and swords mounted in the hall and up the staircase, the main appointments supplied by the colony were chairs—seven of mahogany in the parlor, four with leather bottoms in the pantry, nineteen in the ballroom, sixteen more in walnut in the supper room, and "4 very old black Leather Chairs" in the attic passage. The "Virg.ᵃ" stamp on an armchair in the Daughters of the American Revolution Museum in Washington, D. C., documents the only identified surviving piece of standing furniture at the Palace. There were also a few tables, notably a "Side Board with Marble Slab" in the dining room, and various odds and ends like money scales, leather buckets, and flower pots.

The mixture of new and old furnishings at the Palace also arose from personal transactions between outgoing and incoming governors. Botetourt bought over £700 worth of second-hand furniture from the estate of his predecessor, Francis Fauquier. Some of it was for his dining room—"2 Leather Smok^g Chairs," a "Mahog^y Library Table," an "Oval look^g Glass," and possibly a small reading desk, a dining table, and twelve side chairs.

The aesthetic unity present in virtually all eighteenth-century design no doubt gave the Palace furnishings and their settings the appearance of harmony despite their potpourri of styles. Scholars of the decorative arts may quibble over terms like baroque and rococo, early and late Georgian, or William and Mary, Queen Anne, and Chippendale, and there are indeed significant differences between them. But all European and American art in the period 1700 to 1750 employed visual forms that were principally curvilinear and often were embellished with naturalistic ornaments, mainly foliage, flowers, and shells. Not until Botetourt's time had sophisticated artistic sensibilities developed a taste for straight lines, geometric forms, and antique ornament.

The dominant eighteenth-century decorative taste was best explained to English readers in a book called the *Analysis of Beauty* by William Hogarth, published in 1753. Hogarth described the essence of beauty as "the waving line of variety." He saw a symphony of graceful lines everywhere he looked—in the human body, in commonplace objects, and in nature itself with its "winding walks and serpentine rivers." Others had different thoughts about the beauty of the waving line. Isaac Ware, whose observations on architecture have been cited earlier, grumbled that "the style consists in crooked lines like Cs

Curving lines create a variety of rhythmic patterns in the form and ornament of the silver tablewares in the pantry.

Naturalistic renderings of flowers and foliage harmonize with curving forms. This antique Indian cotton chintz was the prototype for the reproduction bed hangings in his lordship's bedchamber.

Twelve "green bamboo chairs with check'd cushions" were divided between two bedchambers, suggesting that the rooms were furnished as a suite and demonstrating the international inspiration of their design.

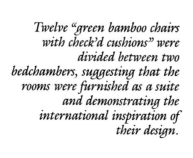

[which] . . . inverted, turned and hooked together, take the place of Greek and Roman elegance. . . . Not because the possessor thinks there is or can be elegance in such fond, weak, ill-jointed and unmeaning figures: it is usually because it is French." Leaving aside national rivalries in commerce, arms, or design and ignoring the early popularity of "the French style" in England and the somewhat later preference for the "gout Anglaise" in France, eighteenth-century people appreciated organic curvilinear forms along with several forms of classical design.

Kings and noblemen spent lavish sums on objects that used costly materials and required many hours of skilled labor to produce. Such high fashion creations were neither desirable nor affordable to the broader spectrum of society, whether French, English, or American. Most people usually preferred conservative versions of high style furniture. They valued quality materials and skillful craftsmanship, work that eighteenth-century consumers termed "neat." They appreciated the appearance of relatively simple

The large black forms of the two cast iron stoves are covered with both rococo and neoclassical ornament, a fairly common combination of styles in the second half of the eighteenth century.

Lord Botetourt's "Sheffield ware tea kitchen" in the new and less costly silverplate was undoubtedly of this late rococo form.

Compared to the complex ornament on the stove and tea kitchen, the design of these silver and silver gilt tablewares is simple and restrained.

forms and restrained ornament, an aesthetic they praised as "plain." Americans shared this preference. If they splurged, it was more likely to be in their choice of accessories. Tablewares, lighting devices, and ornamental knickknacks were often among the showiest statements of the same aesthetic ideal. Fashionable taste expressed principally in a "neat and plain" manner, but here and there flamboyantly, sums up the appearance of the Palace reception rooms.

Many furnishings in the Palace display Hogarth's waving line of variety. Most of the chairs have backs raised on curving uprights. The pierced splats of some are a fretwork of interlacing scrolls. Cabriole or S-shaped legs support with little apparent effort objects as various as tables and tea urns. Plate rims twist and turn. The branching arms of candelabra, globe lamps,

Tradition in the Galt family of Williamsburg maintains that this mahogany desk
and bookcase was also purchased at the
Dunmore sale. It is attributed on the basis
of style and construction to the shop of
Williamsburg cabinetmaker Anthony
Hay, circa 1771–1775.

35

and the patterns of fabrics display the lilting, languid line. Everywhere one looks, one is witness to the truth of the 1766 English play that observed, "Ay, there's none of your strait lines here—but all taste—zig-zag—crinkum-crankum—in and out—right and left—so and again—twisting and turning like a worm."

This curvilinear aesthetic, however playful, was always restrained by the canons of classicism that gave basic structure to all design in the eighteenth century. The most sophisticated decorative arts objects carefully adhered to classical proportions. Many more were merely embellished with decorative motifs inspired by Roman models. Various orders of columns show up frequently. Shells, rosettes, curving foliage, and hanging garlands of fruit, flowers, and ribbons had an ancient history that eighteenth-century designers deliberately recalled.

French curves and other fanciful conceptions were superimposed on the bedrock of classicism. The gothic taste, which had a few passionate English adherents, was almost unknown in America, but the asymmetrical art of the Orient was popular on both sides of the Atlantic. Some modest examples of the oriental taste were to be found in the eighteenth-century Palace. For instance, Botetourt furnished both east bedchambers with bamboo chairs. These exotic expressions were more whimsical and frivolous than deep-rooted and sober. One writer railed against both. Gothic carvings he called "unmeaning," and Chinese figures he declared "resemble nothing in God's creation" and advised "a prudent nation would prohibit [them] for the sake of pregnant women."

Fifteen years later, when Botetourt came to Virginia, people of fashion had grown tired of both the curvilinear style and imitations of Chinese design. Something new was wanted. Designers in England, notably the brothers Adam, captured the public's imagination by inventing yet another reinterpretation of the angular forms and restrained ornament of ancient Roman art and architecture. Botetourt brought with him or later ordered from England some of the first few examples of furnishings exhibiting this new neoclassical aesthetic. In the ballroom his new bright blue wallpaper was a fashionable attention getter. The original Buzaglo stove, from which the design of the two reproductions in the ballroom and supper room have been taken, combines neoclassical swags and urns with older curvilinear features. The original stove is an important artifact because it is one of the first to document the appearance of these stylistic features in the American colonies as early as 1770. Other items in the

This clothespress is signed "J.S." for John Selden, a cabinetmaker of Norfolk, Virginia, and is dated 1775. Loaned to Colonial Williamsburg by Mr. and Mrs. C. Hill Carter, Jr., the press is virtually identical to a design in Thomas Chippendale's Gentleman and Cabinetmaker's Director. *Selden sold a group of furnishings for the Palace to the Commonwealth of Virginia in 1776 during Patrick Henry's governorship.*

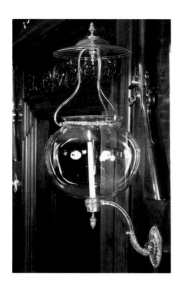

Sixteen "large globe lamps" with brass arms and fittings illuminated the first and second floor halls and the intervening stairs.

neoclassical taste exhibited in the Palace today include the gilt cups on the dining room table, the Sheffield tea kitchen in the little middle room, and carpets reproduced from Adam designs.

Two hundred years ago the Palace was furnished with things both imported and locally made. Virginia's participation in the British colonial empire and the relatively small size of its population of customers for luxury goods help explain which items were produced in the colony and which were ordered from abroad. British mercantile regulations set restrictions on colonial production of manufactured goods; colonies were expected to supply Britain with raw materials and buy its finished products. In theory manufacturing in the colonies was limited to goods intended for a strictly local market. Even without the regulations, the colonial economy could hardly have sustained a full-scale luxury industry. Such looking glasses, cut glass chandeliers, table glass, fashionable metalwares and ceramics, and printed fabrics as were found in well-furnished houses in colonial America were mainly of British manufacture. Much fine furniture, however, was produced locally for nearby customers. England did not regard chair and cabinetmaking establishments as serious threats to worldwide commerce. The scale of their operations and the geographi-

cal limits of their market made their existence tolerable.

Despite its distance from the centers of English taste, Williamsburg boasted a number of cabinetmaking shops that employed craftsmen who were thoroughly conversant with London styles. Information arrived in a variety of ways—with immigrant makers, with imported furniture, and with illustrated books. Carver James Wilson and cabinetmaker William Bucktrout advertised their London origins with pride. Wilson said he could make furniture "carved or plain, after the best Manner," and Bucktrout made "all sorts of cabinetwork, either plain or ornamental, in the neatest and newest fashions." Three craftsmen came from England as members of Governor Botetourt's household, and the upholsterer and gilder, Joseph Kidd, later set himself up in business in Williamsburg. The furniture and furnishings that wealthy Virginians admired in the baggage of new governors they could order for themselves custom-made and shipped from London. Such imports were an inspiration to local craftsmen, although they seldom copied them slavishly. Illustrated books and decorative prints

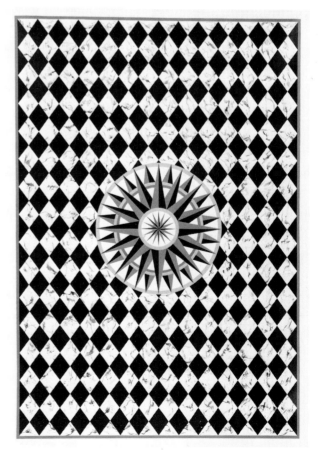

The floorcloth shown in the dining room in the summer was inventoried as "1 large oyl cloth at Mr Kids." The design has been copied from the 1775 trade card of an English floorcloth painter.

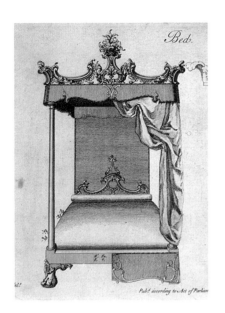

His lordship's bedchamber contained a mahogany bedstead with "chintz and green sattin furniture," probably the one Botetourt purchased for £25 from his predecessor, Governor Fauquier. It was by far the most expensive bed in Fauquier's household. The Virginia-made mahogany bedstead retained its original yellow pine pulley lath for holding up drapery curtains. A design from Chippendale's Director *illustrates how such a bed was properly hung and gives testament to the upholsterer's art.*

sold in Williamsburg were yet another source of fashion. At least one important book of designs written especially for cabinetmakers was owned by a Williamsburg craftsman. The appraisers of cabinetmaker Edmund Dickinson's estate found a copy of "Chippendales Designs" in his library and assigned it the high value of six pounds. Identified as the 1754 edition of Thomas Chippendale's *The Gentleman and Cabinetmaker's Director,* it left its mark on many examples of local furniture. The engraved plates illustrate a variety of designs in the French curvilinear fashion. Most are ornate but a substantial number are simple in the "neat and plain" style. The *Director*'s influence can be seen in several pieces of Virginia furniture exhibited in the Palace. Colonial Williamsburg's curators and conservators used it again in reproducing the carved cornice on the antique bed now in his lordship's chamber.

Artifacts, of course, never arrange themselves. People put them where they need them. Different uses result in different arrangements—some very curious to our modern way of thinking. Because the Botetourt inventory lists the Palace furnishings in the rooms where they were located at the time the inventory was taken, the document is a curator's natural starting point. But even so comprehensive a list of objects is not by itself a furnishing plan. Without explicit evidence for the placement of furniture at the Palace—and none has come to light—curators have had to make inferences from a variety of records pertaining to comparable residences in England and in other colonies.

Available evidence indicates that furniture was mostly ranged along the walls in the eighteenth century. The area in the middle of a room was left open until the space was to be used. Then various tables and a necessary number of chairs or other furniture were brought out and set up for whatever function was intended. Where servants were plentiful these stage set changes could be performed quickly and efficiently. A Palace footman could rapidly transform a parlor from a waiting room into a room for card playing during a ball or other entertainment. He easily could carry a tea table and tea tray anywhere they were wanted—to the parlor, to an upstairs bedchamber, to the dining room, or even to the garden.

If some Palace rooms had multiple uses whose requirements for equipment were met by moving furniture around, other rooms had several functions that called for large and presumably stationary pieces of furniture. The sideboard and dining table, logical items for the dining room, kept company with a writing table, a library table, and a desk. The room was both a place of business and a place for taking meals. The upper middle room was an elegant space for the reception of official visitors. It also doubled as a storage-dressing room. Some of Lord Botetourt's extensive

To fulfill an inventory reference to a carpet in the parlor, a Wilton carpet was woven to an antique paper pattern from the Victoria and Albert Museum in London. The pattern was designed by Anna Maria Garthwaite, one of the few female textile designers in eighteenth-century England.

wardrobe was kept in two mahogany clothespresses standing along the walls.

That such arrangements seem unfamiliar today accentuates our sense of the differences between the past and the present. Insofar as possible the reconstruction offers a "total picture" of Palace life in the eighteenth century, its physical setting, its inhabitants, and the personal, social, political, and business activities that took place there. Yet the fragmentary nature of the evidence and the fallible skills of the historians who study it make it clear that the "total picture" can never be truly complete or accurate. Much of the past has vanished. The rest modern scholars interpret as best they can in an effort to make the past vivid and informative to the visiting public. The Palace and its furnishings preserve patterns of use and consequently a memory of the users. Visitors touring the Palace are encouraged to imagine a family sitting down to tea, a sea captain calling for a Mediterranean pass, an Indian emissary receiving a token of the English king's esteem, a footman opening the door, the butler keeping accounts, a member of the Virginia Council seeking favors, the cook scolding a scullery maid, a neighbor's servant bringing a gift of fresh garden vegetables, a coachman hitching up the horses and carriage. Each person, each vignette, is a piece of the picture of eighteenth-century life at the Palace as Colonial Williamsburg invites you to come to know it.

In 1710 the Virginia legislature recommended a furnishings plan to make the governor's new residence "convenient as well as Ornamental." They specified that "the great Room in the second story be furnished with gilt Leather hangings, [and] two large looking glasses with the Arms of the Colony on them." The glass luster subsequently became part of the colony's decoration. Such trappings lent an aura of tradition and grandeur to this room where it is believed the governor's Council met on occasion.

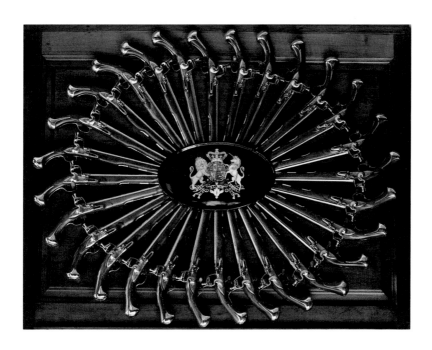

A Tour of the Governor's Palace

"Hall and Passage below"

The Palace door opens on a spectacle of Old World authority and power. The coats of arms proclaim that it is British; the
polished arms declare that it has teeth. It inspired, it impressed, it overawed. Deliberately. Herein dwelt the king of
England's personal representative.

There are many contemporary references to the display of
swords, pistols, and bayoneted muskets in the Palace. William
Byrd II of Westover plantation met Governor Spotswood at
the Palace in 1711 before it was occupied and reported in his
diary that he had seen "several of the Governor's contrivances,
and particularly that for hanging the arms." A century later an
aging St. George Tucker recalled that "a considerable number
of muskets, etc. was always to be seen in the Entrance of the
Palace, where they were arranged upon the walls in an ornamental Manner, as in the Tower of London."

The actual number of arms kept in the Palace "Hall and
Passage below" and extending up the stairs changed from time
to time, but a tally taken in 1750 can be considered as typical:
276 muskets, 100 carbines, 193 pistols, and 264 swords.
Those weapons saw action in skirmishes on the frontier in
1758. Most of the time, however, they were displayed in a
decorative manner suggesting the precision and discipline of a
successful military organization and a great world power. The
curators at Colonial Williamsburg have combined antique and
reproduction firearms and swords in the present display,
which includes 201 muskets (162 with bayonets), 229 pistols,
and 198 swords. They are arranged according to surviving
designs of the period, such as those drawn by John Harris,

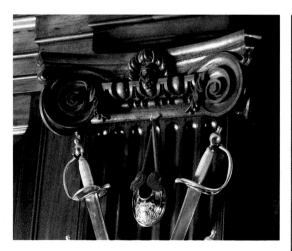

who was responsible for the display in the Tower of London mentioned by St. George Tucker. They also follow the only known domestic arrangement of eighteenth-century arms to have survived in its original form. It is in an English house in Kent called Chevening.

Other notable furnishings in the entrance hall include the damask upholstered chairs and the matched set of globe lamps. Botetourt purchased the chairs from Governor Fauquier's estate. Because the upholstery fabric was the best sort, the chairs were expensive. Careful housekeeping protected the stuffed seats and backs under red checked slipcovers that might have been removed only on ceremonial occasions. The ten lamps installed by Botetourt were the latest fashion in England and in Virginia. Those here are reproduced after some that Thomas Chippendale provided for a house in England in 1771.

The Palace stood as a symbol of British rule over all Virginians, but in keeping with the hierarchical social system of the times, not all Virginians received equal treatment at the door. Probably most people who had business to conduct with the crown's representative completed their transactions in the offices in the east advance building. Even those who requested an audience with the governor or whose rank entitled them to be admitted as guests were given varied receptions according to their social status. A footman escorted prominent citizens to the parlor to wait until the governor could see them. Others waited more publicly and with less comfort in the hall, which Isaac Ware described in his *Complete Body of Architecture* as "an anti-chamber in which people of business, or of the second rank, wait and amuse themselves."

Parlor

Eighteenth-century architectural books and diaries tell us that the furnishings listed in the Botetourt inventory in the "front parlor," the room to the right of the hall, were used in several ways. A parlor near the entrance was a waiting room, a place of business, and a setting for polite entertainment. Isaac Ware noted that a room next to the hall "might very conveniently be made a waiting room for those persons who are of better rank than to be left in the hall." Such persons of quality as were shown into the parlor at the Governor's Palace found there "34 Scripture Prints" to edify them as they waited. To us this may seem like curious waiting room reading material, but the tastes of educated people were different in the colonial era. The diarist Philip Fithian, from whom we learn so much about plantation life in eighteenth-century Virginia, noted in March 1774 that he had "spent much of this Day in Mr Carters Library among the works of mighty-Men; I turned over *Calmets*, Scripture prints, they are beautiful, and vastly entertaining."

The original prints and chairs in the parlor were part of the "standing furniture" owned by the colony. The seven side chairs seen in the room today are adaptations of a rare armchair stamped "Virg.ᵃ" on the seat rail, an indication of its official ownership.

Lord Dunmore originally owned this silver candelabrum, made by Edward Vincent of London in 1759/60 and engraved with the governor's armorials.

The furnishings in the parlor illustrate not only the room's versatility but also the eighteenth-century taste for pairs and sets—two smoking chairs, two card tables, two looking glasses, thirty-four scripture prints, and eleven Chelsea china figures.

Because Botetourt had an interest in collecting live birds and ornithological specimens, curators chose to represent the "11 Chelsea China figures" inventoried as his own personal property with a set of porcelain birds produced at the Chelsea factory near London. Quail, partridge, whippoorwill, and others in the set were modeled and painted after plates in the last volume of George Edwards's *A Natural History of Uncommon Birds* (1743–1751). Like the prints in the parlor and many other objects throughout the Palace, porcelain figurines were available in sets. Suites of matched artifacts, appropriately arranged, were much esteemed in interiors arranged in the grand manner.

Servants easily could transform the waiting room into a place of entertainment by opening the card tables. The night Philip Fithian attended a ball at the Lees' plantation he "was introduced into a small Room where a number of Gentlemen were playing Cards." He added that "all did not join in the Dance for there were parties in Rooms made up, some at Cards; some drinking for Pleasure; some toasting the Sons of america; some singing 'Liberty Songs' as they call'd them." Obviously the latter were unlikely to have been heard at the Palace, but no doubt on occasion its rooms rang with other words and melodies.

Pantry

The footman stationed at the door and all other Palace servants came under the supervision of the butler who, from the evidence of the Botetourt inventory, managed the entire household from his office in the pantry where he sat on a stool before a library table. Other furnishings in the room suggest that William Marshman, Botetourt's loyal butler, slept and dressed there as well. The "Ticken couch" was supplied with bedding, and the room

was equipped with a "Wash hand bason, bottle and stand." Marshman's personal possessions, which of course would not have been listed in his master's inventory, might have been stored in a "Mahog^y Beaureau."

The pantry provided the butler with a secure and strategic place to carry out his responsibilities. Accounts can be kept most anywhere, but staff supervision and security for valuables require a physical presence at a particular place. Jefferson's plan of the Palace shows two doors into the pantry. Although probably they rarely stood open, they gave Marshman direct access to the comings and goings in the hall and to activities in the little middle room, the kitchen, and other service areas.

According to Botetourt's inventory, over 1,600 items, many made of silver, were stored in the pantry. The plate probably was kept behind solid, well-locked doors. Marshman's presence in the pantry night and day provided additional security, and he kept "2 braces of pocket pistols" there for enforcement. Today a comparable collection of antique plate is housed in locked glass cupboards that remind us of the importance of security but also permit modern visitors to see the rows on rows of platters and silver sauceboats. Other items stored in the pantry—an assortment of candles, wines and spirits, and the decanters and accompanying glasswares—were not so valuable as the plate, but they too needed to be removed from the temptation of casual visitors and temporary servants. From their place of safekeeping in the pantry the consumables and plate were issued as needed.

William Marshman, Lord Botetourt's butler, kept a watchful eye over the silver, glassware, and other supplies stored in the pantry.

49

Little Middle Room

Servants who set and waited on table must have used the little middle room as a staging area. The dishes stored in the closet were mainly items associated with the preparation, serving, and consumption of beverages and light refreshments. Tea kettles, teapots, slop basins, cream pots, sugar basins, coffeepots, chocolate pots, hand mills for coffee and chocolate, cups and saucers, lemon strainers, and lime squeezers were all found there with waiters and tea trays and even a "Scallop'd claw tea table." Robert Dodsley, whose prescriptions for masters and servants have been quoted elsewhere, also wrote a rhymed description of a footman's life. *The Muse in Livery* (1732) described preparations that footmen must have busied themselves with in the little middle room:

> The time of drinking tea comes on.
> The kettle fill'd, the water boil'd,
> The cream provided, biscuits pil'd,
> The lamp prepar'd; I strait engage
> The Lilliputian equipage
> Of dishes, saucers, spoons, and tongs,
> And all th' Et cetera which thereto belongs.
> Which rang'd in order and decorum,
> I carry in, and set before 'em;
> Than pour a Green, or Bohea out,
> And, as commanded, hand about.

In cold weather the Palace's many fireplaces and its two extraordinary freestanding stoves provided warmth. Servants secured the necessary wood and coal, laid and tended the fires, and polished the stoves, grates, andirons, tongs, shovels, and fenders. Permanently installed in the fireplace of this room and in those of the library and dining room are fashionable neoclassical stove grates that probably burned only coal. Four other fireplaces are equipped with portable coal grates that burned either coal or wood. Andirons for wood were used elsewhere.

The closet in the little middle room held blue and white tea wares, which the Botetourt accounts specified as "Nankeen China," a Chinese export porcelain. Using the china tea service and silver stored in the pantry, such as the large tea board and the "Sheffield ware tea kitchen," or hot water urn, the staff could prepare a handsome tea tray for the governor and his guests.

Powder Room

Fashionable dress in the eighteenth century required that gentlemen wear wigs. They were expensive to buy and needed continual curling and powdering to maintain them. In large houses such activities were performed in special "powdering rooms." Although the powder room in the Governor's Palace contained "1 Wig block with Screw Stands," the room's function can only be guessed at. It also held two copper coal scuttles, a stone cistern with a brass cock, a small wire cage, and other odds and ends that had nothing to do with wigs. "2 Powder Machins" and "26 lb common hair powder" and "27 lb best do," which one might have expected to find in a powder room, were kept instead in a storeroom on the third floor.

Staircase and Passage Upstairs

Available evidence reveals that several governors used both the ground floor dining room and the middle room upstairs as offices. For some visitors on state business to the Palace, the stairs and the passage on the second floor were another stage in their progress toward an audience with the royal governor. The most important callers probably were shown immediately to the chairs outside the upper middle room where they waited for the governor to receive them. Those who had been waiting in the hall or parlor knew that their turn had finally come when a footman led them upstairs. Although Botetourt's inventory calls it a "passage," the space was furnished as an antechamber, described by Thomas Sheraton in the *Cabinet Directory* as "A room that leads to the principal apartment where servants wait, or strangers, till they may be spoken to by those on whom they attend."

The way to his lordship's presence was lined with further displays of arms and lighted by additional globe lamps. The mahogany chairs are reproductions based on a Williamsburg-made example with a Spotswood family history. The paintings are antique equivalents of the original "3 large Roman Catholick Pictures" that imbued this executive waiting area with somber dignity.

Globe lamps at regular intervals and a continuing display of arms in an ornamental arrangement enhance the sense of ceremonial procession for important visitors to the middle room on the second floor.

The governor often conducted official business in the upper middle room. Elegant looking glasses, crimson damask, and substantial mahogany furniture underscore the room's ceremonial character.

Middle Room Upstairs

As the culmination of this carefully staged sequence of advancing and waiting, the visitor was ushered into the presence of his lordship in a large room deliberately furnished to heighten its ceremonial effect. The passage and the "middle room" divided the second floor into two suites. The bachelor Botetourt reserved the smaller rooms on the west side of the house for his library and bedroom; the eastern rooms probably accommodated his guests. Although other governors undoubtedly used the bedchambers differently according to family requirements, the middle room was always the place where the governor conducted official business. The "seal of the Colony" is among the items listed here. Like other Palace rooms, however, the middle room did double duty, as a parlor and perhaps as a dressing room.

The presence of "2 Mahog^y cloaths presses with apparel" and "1 Wash Bason Mahog. stand compleat" poses an interpretive problem. In the eighteenth century people of wealth and importance received visitors and

The Botetourt inventory reveals that "the Seal of the Colony" was kept in this room. Issued by the crown, the silver matrices were used to form the large wax seals that were attached to and authenticated certain official documents.

The presence of a washstand and clothespresses with wearing apparel indicates that Lord Botetourt used this room for other than official purposes.

petitioners in a curious ritual called a *levee*. For the host or hostess the event might include the time-consuming process of dressing fashionably. Some colonial governors may have used the upper middle room adjoining their bedchambers for this purpose, but Botetourt customarily dressed very early in the morning before taking his daily walk to the college chapel where he attended seven o'clock morning prayers. If he indulged in levees, they were rare or occasional events.

A proposal presented to the Assembly about 1710 "for rendering the New House convenient as well as Ornamental" recommended that "the great Room in the second Story be furnished with gilt Leather hangings, 16 chairs of the same, [and] two large looking glasses with the Arms of the Colony on them according to the new Mode. Two small Tables to stand under the Looking Glasses and two Marble Tables Eight Glass sconces four Chimney Glasses for the said floor." Clearly a grand appearance was intended. Whether the proposal was acted on is unknown, but in 1770 the colony—not the governor—owned three looking glasses and a glass luster, or chandelier, in the middle room. Botetourt's personal property included the clothespresses and the washstand, the fireplace equipment, three mahogany tables, a desk and bookcase, and "1 large Chimney Glass gilt carv'd frame and 4 Gilded brackets."

Library

Printing and publishing expanded rapidly in the eighteenth century, contributing to the development of the library as a large room where all family members could gather to pursue leisure reading and writing. The library of the Palace followed the earlier practice whereby a gentleman kept his books in a small room, which was often connected to his bedchamber. The bachelor Botetourt may not have minded the older arrangement, but his taste in books and library furnishings was decidedly up to date. His inventory includes several of the new novels like *Tom Jones* and

The library, or study, today contains 85 percent of the titles listed in the Botetourt inventory. Prints of great men were considered suitably edifying for a library, as were maps such as this one of North and South America.

The Adventures of Joseph Andrews in addition to traditional sermons, histories, legal treatises, and geographical descriptions.

The current refurbishing employs several features that are well documented both to the eighteenth century in general and to the Palace in particular. Venetian blinds, wall-to-wall carpeting, dust curtains to protect the books, and prints in frames hung with brass nails emulate eighteenth-century practices. Botetourt's inventory does not mention a chair in this room. Although one easily could have been brought from around the corner for reading and writing, it is also possible that Botetourt had a writing desk like the one Robert Carter installed in his schoolroom—"so high that the writers must stand."

His Lordship's Bedchamber

Botetourt's inventory indicates that he used his bedchamber for sleeping and dressing. He purchased the mahogany bedstead with its "Chintz and green sattin furniture and 1 bed carpet" from the estate of Governor Fauquier along with other furnishings in the room. In the "large Walnut chest of draws" and the "Mahog^y dress^g table" he kept that part of his extensive wardrobe which was not stored in the middle room or in the chamber over the dining room. Like men of fashion in the eighteenth century generally, Botetourt was a clotheshorse. His drawers overflowed with fifty-six ruffled shirts, one hundred fifty-two pairs of stockings in many different colors, thirty-six pairs of shoes, boots, and pumps in addition to coats, waistcoats, and "britches" in a marvelous variety of fabrics—from black velvet and silks of crimson, blue, and white to gold and silver lace.

The antique Virginia bed retains a rare feature, pulleys in the lath. Cords suspended from the pulleys draw the curtains into graceful folds. The fabric, a reproduction of an eighteenth-century mordant-painted cotton, also covers the carved cornice in the manner of the times. Green gauze is used for summer mosquito netting, which Botetourt certainly needed and is known to have had. The restored bed's appearance, both summer and winter, closely follows an engraving in Chippendale's *Director.*

The seasonal mosquito hangings were listed in a third floor closet as "2 Venitian Suits of Gauze Curtains."

Nail holes on the surviving pulley lath indicated that the bedstead originally had a cornice. The re-created cut through cornice is an adaptation of a modest design in the Director.

The bed posts had holes for brass cloak pins needed to tie off the lines that pull up the curtains.

His lordship's bed in its summer guise is hung with silk mosquito curtains.

63

Chamber over the Parlor

Lord Botetourt probably used the two bedrooms on the east side of the Palace as a guest suite. The *Virginia Gazette* records that he entertained Governor William Tryon of North Carolina with his wife and daughter for about a month in 1769 and Governor Robert Eden of Maryland and his wife for a shorter time in 1770. Household accounts suggest that house guests frequently enjoyed the governor's hospitality. Still, we know less than we would like about the rooms in which they stayed; architectural books of the period comment mainly on public spaces.

A combination of evidence from the Botetourt inventory, other contemporary sources, and surviving decorative schemes in other English and American houses provided sufficient precedents for an authentic refurnishing plan. The inventory refers to "Green Bamboo chairs with check cushions" in both chambers and in the larger one to "green stuf window Curtains and rods." When refurnishing the Palace, the curators were therefore encouraged to adopt a uniform color scheme for the suite as a whole, but with different accents in each room. The practice of highlighting

During the occupancy of Lord Botetourt, the chamber over the parlor and the chamber over the dining room were used as guest rooms. This east side of the second floor, with a closet between the two chambers, could form a convenient suite. The bedstead in this room was dressed in "a suit of white callico Curtains and valens, . . . and white Virg^a cloth counterpane."

architectural details with contrasting paint colors was known both in England and in fashionable American houses of the period.

Reproduction oak bedsteads with full sets of hangings in reproduction fabrics dominate the furnishing arrangement of both rooms. Because bed frames and valances were either painted or concealed by the curtains and spread, the original cabinetmaker worked with oak, which cost less than mahogany. Both beds are described in the inventory in ways that recall George Hepplewhite's remarks in the *Cabinet-Maker and Upholsterer's Guide* (1788). Beds, says the text, are elegant, expensive, available in a "variety of shapes," and can be hung with "almost every stuff which the loom produces." In this room the bed hangings follow the inventory description of a "Suit of white callico Curtains . . . and white Virg^a cloth counterpane."

The other furniture is antique and conforms to furniture in the inventory. Especially noteworthy is the clothespress signed by John Selden of Norfolk and dated 1775. It closely resembles a "neat and plain" design in Chippendale's *Director*. All the colony's standing furniture in this room hung on the walls—a looking glass and fourteen prints. Glass transfers depicting the twelve months and portraits of King George III and Queen Charlotte have been chosen to represent the latter.

The colony owned the fourteen prints—shown here as glass transfers—that decorated the walls of the chamber over the parlor.

Closet

Separating the two east chambers is a small cubicle designated in the inventory as a closet. It was furnished as a dressing room with a wash basin on a mahogany stand and a "large deal toilet table." Like the choice of oak for the bedsteads, the use of deal (the English term for pine or fir) for the table implies a fabric covering. On two different occasions upholsterer Joseph Kidd billed Botetourt for dressing a toilet table. The framed prints and the looking glass in the closet were property of the colony, as were similar objects in the next room. The series of prints entitled "Gods in Love," which was chosen to furnish the closet, was first published in 1708, remained popular throughout the eighteenth century, and is known to have been owned in Virginia.

"The Gods in Love" was a popular set of prints first issued in 1708. John Custis of Virginia owned a set in 1717, so they were chosen to represent the "10 Prints in Frames in the Closet."

Chamber over the Dining Room

To us it seems curious that the only personal use Lord Botetourt made of this, the largest chamber in the Palace, was to store more of his clothing in a mahogany clothespress. Perhaps he reasoned that convenience and hospitality required him to accommodate guests in the larger room and its adjoining suite. The arrangement was particularly sensible when gentlemen like Governors Tryon and Eden were accompanied by their wives. With so many Palace rooms devoted to official business, housekeeping, and storage, there was little space left for a female guest to find privacy. On the occasions when women used these east side chambers, servants undoubtedly adapted them for the purpose by bringing in tea tables, needlework frames, or writing desks.

The large mahogany desk and bookcase that closely resembles several other large case pieces was made, the curators believe, in Williamsburg. Its sound history of local ownership includes a traditional association with the Palace. The oak bed is hung with a reproduction purple and white copperplate print showing classical ruins in a landscape. The lining is green silk. Thomas Chippendale used this color combination in the 1760s, and Hepplewhite suggested that with a dark colored pattern "a green silk lining may be used with good effect." Neoclassical ruins remind us of the fashionable eighteenth-century interest in the buildings of antiquity. The geometric pattern of the Wilton cut-pile reproduction bed carpet appealed to the same taste. The pattern and the carpet's U-shape—it surrounds but does not extend under the bed—are based on a surviving carpet Robert Adam designed in 1767 for Osterley Park, a house near London.

The room over the dining room is furnished as a guest chamber. The holster and three-cornered hatbox are items typically carried by travelers in the eighteenth century.

Staircase and Passage Downstairs

The staircase leads downward to the dining room and ballroom, whose doors are enhanced with plaques painted with the royal arms and framed above by fans of matched pistols.

Dining Room

In their architectural book of 1773 Robert and James Adam wrote that "the eating rooms are considered as the apartments of conversation, in which we are to pass a great part of our time." At the Governor's Palace and at several other large Virginia houses of the period, the dining room was a place to eat, to talk, and to conduct business. Evidence suggests that Botetourt's predecessor, Governor Fauquier, furnished the room for these multiple purposes, an arrangement that Botetourt found congenial as well, judging from the furniture recorded here in the inventory. A writing table in walnut, a desk, and a mahogany library table were provided for business. The library table is fully described in one of the Botetourt manuscripts as "a large and very neat mahogany lybery table of very fine wood covered with leather the moulding richly carved on 8 3-wheel casters." Valued at £24, it probably was the most expensive item in the room with the possible exception of the six gold cups.

The dining equipment included large and small mahogany dining tables and a "Side Board with Marble Slab," a plate warmer, and a wine cooler. The table is set for dessert with silver gilt plates, knives and forks, gold cups, some "ornamental china," a glass pyramid, cut glass, and fine table linen.

The two "smoking chairs," today more commonly called "corner chairs," are reproductions based on a Virginia prototype. The twelve mahogany chairs with modern horsehair upholstery that form a set are antique and were acquired because chairs of this design can be associated with considerable assurance with Dunmore and perhaps with Botetourt. Today four similar chairs are at Badminton House in Gloucestershire, the seat of Botetourt's heir. The typically north of England or Scottish form relates to Dunmore's Scottish origins. Furthermore, a similar chair with a good Dunmore history is privately owned in Virginia.

Window curtains were taken down and the carpet was replaced with a painted floorcloth during the summer months.

Glassware in the kitchen included "21 Glass Salvers" and "1 plain [glass pyramid] with 14 pails" as well as dozens of sweetmeat, jelly, and syllabub glasses. They create an impressive and glittering centerpiece on the table, which is set for dessert.

Items both decorative and useful complete the furnishings. Botetourt ordered some fire screens with maps on them. The rare example here with a history of Botetourt ownership is on loan from Kenmore Association, Inc. Hanging on the chimney breast is a Virginia map, the work of John Henry, Patrick Henry's surveyor father. Botetourt helped the elder Henry secure a royal patent to further the map's publication, and he bought a copy for £10. The inventory mentions "11 Chelsea China Figures" represented on the mantel by masqueraders of the gold anchor period. In displaying "13 Wax portraits," Botetourt was following the fashion of the 1760s. Popular subjects were members of the royal family, religious leaders, and philosophers. Botetourt himself sat for a wax portrait by Isaac Gossett, a leading London modeler. It was the likeness later used for the posthumous public statue and for additional copies in wax ordered by various Virginia gentlemen as personal mementoes of the popular governor.

Eighteenth-century cookbooks and etiquette manuals set down the procedure for formal dining. An important meal included several courses, each featuring a

The marble sideboard table holds a punch bowl, wine bottle and decanters, and some of Botetourt's "28 cut wine glasses." Footmen kept diners well supplied with spirits. Gentlemen were expected to practice the gracious art of toasting as part of the dining ritual.

wide variety of dishes. All were arranged symmetrically on the main table with the principal meat dish positioned in front of the host or hostess who carved it ceremoniously. Servants helped distribute the food and stood by to carry glasses to the sideboard where they were rinsed and refilled. A separate dessert course, requiring its own assortment of dishes, concluded the meal.

Toasting was an important part of mealtime ritual at wealthy Virginia tables. In February 1774 at Robert Carter's plantation, Philip Fithian recorded, "Toasts after Dinner, the *King. Queen.* Absent Friends, Governor of Virginia, and his Lady just arrived, and Success to American Trade and Commerce." Historians presume that at the end of a long meal Virginia practice followed the English custom that required ladies to retire to a parlor, leaving the gentlemen to drink and talk around the dining table. The Adam brothers described this social practice and related it to political discussions.

> Every person of rank here is either a member of the legislation, or entitled by his condition to take part in the political arrangements of his country, and to enter with ardour into those discussions to which they give rise; these circumstances lead men to live more with one another, and more detached from the society of ladies. The eating rooms are considered as the apartments of conversation, in which we are to pass a great part of our time.

The Palace dining room furnishings suggest not only after dinner conversations but working sessions with pertinent papers within easy reach on the nearby desk.

This Williamsburg-made desk in the dining room, which is attributed to the Anthony Hay shop, belonged to Lord Dunmore. Objects such as this desk, along with other documentation, indicate that governors patronized local tradesmen.

Ballroom

The addition of the ball- and supper rooms off the north side of the Palace about 1753 allowed larger numbers of guests to be accommodated at dinners or balls. One afternoon Botetourt wrote to his superior, Lord Hillsborough, that "52 dined with me yesterday and I expect at least that number today—most of whom [at three in the afternoon] are already arrived and waiting for me." The dining room was too small for such gatherings, but the ball- and supper rooms were spacious and well equipped with "3 large mahog^y dining tables," a "large round walnut do," "2 long walnut dining Tables," plus forty-seven chairs and eight long stools. At balls dancing was the main entertainment. "Routs" were the newly fashionable receptions, which one critic considered an "absurd practice" because instead of seeing one's "friends as they chanced to come," the idea was "to see them all at once, and entertain none of them." Although poorly suited to the gentle art of conversation, routs—like modern cocktail parties—were useful for official entertaining.

Lord Botetourt acquired from London "3 glass lustres [or chandeliers] with 6 branches each" to give added light and elegance to this important social space.

77

The ballroom, as Botetourt redecorated it, made a forceful visual statement. In 1771 Robert Beverley observed that "the Lord Botetourt had hung a room with plain blue paper and bordered it with a narrow stripe of gilt leather, which I thought had a pretty effect." He liked it so much he treated the walls of his own house in a similar manner. Botetourt was also responsible for providing the Palace with portraits of King George III and Queen Charlotte. "I have the satisfaction to find that the King and Queen's pictures are arrived perfectly safe. Mr. Ramsay never did two better. We are all delighted with them." Allan Ramsay, the king's official portrait painter, produced many portraits of the monarchs. Those in the refurnished Palace are his work too, although not the same ones that hung here in Williamsburg in the eighteenth century. The "large dutch" stoves that warmed the otherwise unheated ballroom and supper room were other Botetourt additions. The ones he originally ordered for the Palace have disappeared, but a third stove, which he purchased at the same time for the Capitol, survives and served as a model for the two reproductions. Lord Botetourt lighted the ballroom with his own "3 glass lustres [chandeliers] with 6 branches each" and with the colony's brass candelabra that stood on wall brackets.

Allan Ramsay and his studio produced a large number of distinguished state portraits of King George III and Queen Charlotte for official use in England and throughout the British empire.

Unlike his predecessor, Lord Dunmore is known to have owned a harpsichord and other musical instruments.

Supper Room

The supper room was the second unit in the suite of rooms built for entertaining, and if the practice mentioned by Isaac Ware in his *Complete Body of Architecture* was followed at the Palace, the rooms were "opened only on such occasions." For parties Botetourt's staff laid tables with beautiful dishes and artfully prepared foods that would have given the room a temporary elegance. At the time of Botetourt's death its decorative scheme was clearly due for changes. Botetourt's new stove was in place and the paper, the linen lining, and the border for new wall coverings were on hand, but the paperwork had not yet been completed.

The colony owned the "2 long walnut dining Tables" and the "16 Walnut leather bottom chairs" which, according to the inventory, furnished the space. The present chairs are reproductions of a walnut side chair that retains its original black leather upholstery, has a good history of association with Lord Dunmore at the Palace, and displays visual characteristics and structural details that suggest it was made in Williamsburg. Also on view in the room is a rare chamber organ of the

1770s. Although Botetourt kept no musical instruments at the Palace, he hired musicians when he needed to entertain his guests.

All this splendor was not for everyone's eyes. No governor would have dreamed of inviting the general run of storekeepers, craftsmen, and people of little substance. Governors welcomed as guests to the Palace members of the Council, their families, and other prominent citizens. The *Virginia Gazette* sometimes reported festivities organized to honor the monarch's birthday or occasionally to celebrate special events. If several of these descriptions are pieced together, the full flavor of a "grand Entertainment" emerges from the newsprint. A 1738 account is typical of these reports:

> Last Monday being the Anniversary of His Majesty's Birth Day, was observ'd in this City with all the distinguishing Marks of Loyalty we are capable of shewing. In the Morning the Public Flag was hoisted on the Capitol; at Noon the Cannon at the Governor's House was trebly discharg'd; and at Night most of the Gentlemen's and Other Houses of Note, were illuminated. His Honour the Governor was pleas'd to give a handsome Entertainment for the Gentlemen and Ladies together with a Ball.

The best description of a supper served at a governor's ball in Williamsburg was a *Gazette* story about the celebration of the British victory at the battle

Ornamental china, such as this Derby figure of Bacchus, was often used to decorate a dessert table.

A late evening supper climaxes a festive ball at the Palace. The table is fashionably dressed with an artificial garden on a mirrored plateau.

of Culloden in 1746. Because Governor Gooch was ill, the ball to which he "was pleas'd to contribute very largely" took place at the Capitol.

> A very numerous Company of Gentlemen and Ladies . . . withdrew to Supper [after dancing], there being a very handsome Collation spread on three Tables, in three different Rooms, consisting of near 100 Dishes, after the most delicate Taste. There was also provided a great Variety of the choicest and best Liquors, in which the Healths of the King, the Prince and Princess of Wales, the Duke, and the rest of the Royal Family, the Governor, Success to His Majesty's arms, Prosperity to this Colony, and many other Loyal Healths were chearfully drank.

Meanwhile the general populace milled around the streets and public greens. They enjoyed other parts of the celebration—the flag raising, the cannon salutes, a huge bonfire, and a general illumination of the town. They also had "3 Hogsheads of Punch," which may account for the "unaffected Chearfulness" that "appeared in the Countenance of the Company." That night "the whole Affair was conducted with great Decency and good Order," but probably this was not always true. A short note concluding instructions for the 1727 birthnight party cautions that "all Immaginable care must be taken to prevent disorders and disasters."

The ultimate disorder and disaster for British authority in Virginia came with the American Revolution. Lord Dunmore and his family took flight from the Palace on the night of June 8, 1775. Independence was declared. Although political upheaval did not immediately overthrow the social order, it did establish a foundation on which a different vision of society was conceived. The founders of the new nation were wont to express their conception in the language of philosophy, but their ideas were born of practical experience nurtured in relationships that had developed over many years between people and their governments in the colonies and in Great Britain. Those relationships found symbolic expression in the architecture and furnishings of the Governor's Palace in Williamsburg.

Peace brought the beginning of the end for the old building. In 1781 Timothy Pickering observed the ravages that the Revolution had wreaked on rooms that once "were finished in a rich and costly manner." The remains of the rooms and of Botetourt's richly ornamented state coach inspired some reflections on the Virginians' infatuation with elegance. The coach, he said, "is gilded in every part, even the edges of the tires of the wheels. The arms of Virginia are painted on every side. The motto of the arms [in translation, "Virginia gives a fourth quarter to the world"] led me to remark how peculiarly disposed the Virginians have been to adopt ideas of royalty and magnificence." Display reinforced the governor's vice-regal image of power and authority. By living elegantly he complimented the people he governed. Sheraton had got it right in his *Cabinet Directory*: "The grandeur then introduced . . . is not to be considered, as the ostentatious parade of its proprietor, but the respect he pays to the rank of his visitants."

The Gardens

like the Palace building, the pleasure gardens behind it embodied two approaches to design. Some parts followed classical ideas. In them formality is clearly visible today in the precisely balanced paths and planted beds and trees, the geometrical parterres, the control and confinement provided by the brick walls, the measured progression of the terraces, and the straight lines of the canal. Elsewhere a designing eye and cultivating hand enhanced the landscape's natural qualities. The meandering paths along the

canal and the big open views of the countryside beyond the formal gardens hint at a newer taste for the illusion of artlessness.

Serious proponents of garden design wrote treatises about both visions of the man-made landscape. The preposterous hope of one seventeenth-century advocate of formalism helps us understand how adamant some people were about order and symmetry: "If the sea had been drawn round the earth in regular figures and borders, it might have been a great beauty to our globe." The stars would have been more beautiful "if they had been disposed into regular Figures . . . according to the rules of Art and Symmetry." Only toward the end of the seventeenth century did people begin to appreciate the beauty of untouched nature. Landscape painting, scenic sightseeing, an interest in the asymmetrical aesthetic of oriental art, and naturalistic or English gardening arose from the same impulses. By 1712 *The Spectator* noted that "the Mind of Man naturally hates every thing that looks like a Restraint upon it. [The polite imagination prefers] wide and undetermined Prospects . . . a troubled Ocean, a Heaven adorned with Stars and Meteors."

When Spotswood arrived in Virginia in 1710, the Palace was unfinished and no provision had been made for its grounds. Soon after the House of Burgesses authorized a "Court-yard" on the town side, a walled garden 254 feet by 144 on the north side, and two pairs of "handsome gates [to] be made to the said court-yard and garden." There is also mention of orchards, a kitchen garden, and pasture.

Several times between 1710 and 1720 Spotswood's grandiose gardening plans ran afoul of his Virginia neighbors. Although he secured permission

to cut a vista through land owned by John Custis, the unexpected loss of good building timber angered that miserly misanthrope. Other troubles arose from his easy use of public money. In 1713 the legislature authorized Spotswood to procure such men and materials as were "necessary and convenient for the Compleating and Finishing the Building and work." He told them that he spent about two hundred pounds a year of the colony's money, but, because he served as his own overseer, he argued that he actually saved the public purse one hundred pounds annually. The burgesses were not impressed. Whether the waterworks and falling gardens were the last straw or whether the burgesses simply resented the governor's high-handed treatment, they took him up on his offer to "surrender the Trust and Power, that I am by law posses'd of for Compleating the Governors House." From then on all work at the Palace and on its gardens was firmly controlled by the legislature.

Still, Spotswood was praised for his creative landscaping achievement. In 1737 one writer commended him for "laying out of Ground to the best advantage." Later governors apparently enjoyed the gardens. Shortly after his arrival in Williamsburg in 1727, Governor Gooch described the Palace to his brother: "The house is an excellent one indeed, all manner of conveniences that you can imagine, an handsome garden, an orchard full of fruit, and a very large Park." Erratic maintenance and changes made to the original plan when the ballroom wing was added did not ruin the essential beauty of Spotswood's scheme. It wore well with time. A letter that Lord Botetourt wrote in 1769 contains a brief description of his new surroundings that rings with sincerity: "My house is admirable, the ground behind it is much broke, well planted and watered by beautiful Rills, and the whole in every respect just as I could wish."

The personality of a garden is ephemeral. It changes from season to season and from year to year. The garden Spotswood designed was different from the one that Botetourt knew. The restored garden is beautiful in still other ways. The design of the garden that visitors see today is consistent with such documentary and archaeological evidence as there is and otherwise follows English practice of the period. But no one knows exactly what the Palace garden looked like at any one time in the eighteenth century.

Today geometric compositions of gravel walks and planted beds, outlined with low clipped hedges, lead eye and foot to both principal entrances to the main Palace building. From the entrance on Palace Green, or even better from the balcony above, one can look down a straight path, peripherally see a symmetrical arrangement of oval beds, appreciate the barrier wall with its elegant iron gate, and beyond it follow the straight line of the green. Rows of catalpa trees emphasize the axis. On the north, from the door to the ballroom wing, the eye picks up an orderly progression of avenue and crosswalks. First comes the geometry of the parterre in the foreground, then a change in level marked by three easy steps and a broad cross path, next a fence and a lacy iron gate. Then the axial control relaxes; the grassy lawn appears natural. It ends with a hidden wall that physically but not visually separates the lawn from the wide view of the rural landscape. This sequence of intersecting lines—path and steps, fence, gate, and wall—provides rhythmic and psychological divisions to a composition that moves in controlled stages from formal order to increased naturalism. Both the town side and the country view conform to the ideal of a gentleman's fashionable garden.

Further exploration of the present grounds leads to other features of a carefully planned eighteenth-century estate. Left or west from the ballroom wing are four terraces connected by flights of stairs. On the upper level several openings in the plantings reveal a stream, canal, and ravine. Here taste, knowledge, and labor have transformed nature into an artificial waterway and a picturesque garden. A beguiling arrangement of paths and

a decorative bridge encourage visitors to descend from the terraces and explore the banks. At the end of the canal and a little to the east rises a mound of earth that insulates the original eighteenth-century icehouse. From atop the mount viewers enjoy a pleasant prospect of that part of the garden.

The yards that flank the main buildings were work areas. One served the needs of the inhabitants of the Palace. It included the kitchen, kitchen garden, smokehouse, scullery, and laundry. The other, ringed by barns, stables, and carriage house, provided storage for crops and shelter for animals.

Beyond the Palace and its formal gardens lay an eighteenth-century park, a less ordered private preserve of fields and managed forest. The Palace lands eventually included 364 acres, approximately ten in gardens and service areas around the house and the rest given to park and farmland. The park provided scenic views from the Palace and offered pleasant places to ride and walk. It served also as farmland, orchard, pasture, a source of firewood, and possibly a preserve for deer hunting.

Both formal and natural landscapes appealed to the sensibilities of eighteenth-century Virginians. In his garden a wealthy gentleman acknowledged his English background and demonstrated his awareness of contemporary intellectual ideas and fashionable tastes. For colonists whose forebears had tamed the Virginia wilderness, an appreciation of the beauties of nature and an ability to control it inside garden walls had a special poignancy. For English governors, living in the remote provincial capital of Williamsburg, the Palace park and gardens recalled the "quiet country manner" most were accustomed to at home.